JANUARY 2025

NOTABLE DATES: 1 NEW YEAR'S DAY / 2 NEW YEAR HOLIDAY (SCOTLAND) / 29 LUNAR NEW YEAR (SNAKE)

W	T	F	S	S	M	T	W	T	F	S	S	M	T	W	T	F	S	S	M	T	W	T	F	S	S	M	T	W	T	F
1	2	3	4	5	6	7	8	9	10	11	12	13	14	15	16	17	18	19	20	21	22	23	24	25	26	27	28	29	30	31

SALLY SEES
A FEARFUL VISION

Disney
TIM BURTON'S
THE NIGHTMARE BEFORE CHRISTMAS

FEBRUARY 2025

NOTABLE DATES: 14 VALENTINE'S DAY / 28 RAMADAN BEGINS

S	S	M	T	W	T	F	S	S	M	T	W	T	F	S	S	M	T	W	T	F	S	S	M	T	W	T	F
1	2	3	4	5	6	7	8	9	10	11	12	13	14	15	16	17	18	19	20	21	22	23	24	25	26	27	28

DISNEY
TIM BURTON'S
THE NIGHTMARE BEFORE CHRISTMAS

MARCH 2025

NOTABLE DATES: 1 ST. DAVID'S DAY / 4 SHROVE TUESDAY / 8 INTERNATIONAL WOMEN'S DAY / 17 ST. PATRICK'S DAY / 30 MOTHER'S DAY (UK) & DAYLIGHT SAVING TIME STARTS

S	S	M	T	W	T	F	S	S	M	T	W	T	F	S	S	M	T	W	T	F	S	S	M	T	W	T	F	S	S	M
1	2	3	4	5	6	7	8	9	10	11	12	13	14	15	16	17	18	19	20	21	22	23	24	25	26	27	28	29	30	31

HALLOWEEN TOWN PRESENTS
JACK'S FLOATING HEAD TRICK

DISNEY
TIM BURTON'S
THE NIGHTMARE BEFORE CHRISTMAS

APRIL 2025

NOTABLE DATES: 12 PASSOVER BEGINS / 18 GOOD FRIDAY / 20 EASTER SUNDAY / 21 EASTER MONDAY / 23 ST. GEORGE'S DAY

T	W	T	F	S	S	M	T	W	T	F	S	S	M	T	W	T	F	S	S	M	T	W	T	F	S	S	M	T	W
1	2	3	4	5	6	7	8	9	10	11	12	13	14	15	16	17	18	19	20	21	22	23	24	25	26	27	28	29	30

I HAD THE MOST
TERRIBLE VISION

Disney
TIM BURTON'S
THE NIGHTMARE BEFORE CHRISTMAS

MAY 2025

NOTABLE DATES: 5 EARLY MAY BANK HOLIDAY / 26 SPRING BANK HOLIDAY

T	F	S	S	M	T	W	T	F	S	S	M	T	W	T	F	S	S	M	T	W	T	F	S	S	M	T	W	T	F	S
1	2	3	4	5	6	7	8	9	10	11	12	13	14	15	16	17	18	19	20	21	22	23	24	25	26	27	28	29	30	31

SEE JACK'S AMAZING ASSISTANT
ZERO
LIVE
in a
MAGIC
TRICK!
Disney
TIM BURTON'S
THE NIGHTMARE BEFORE CHRISTMAS

JUNE 2025

NOTABLE DATES: 15 FATHER'S DAY (UK) / 25 ISLAMIC NEW YEAR BEGINS

S	M	T	W	T	F	S	S	M	T	W	T	F	S	S	M	T	W	T	F	S	S	M	T	W	T	F	S	S	M
1	2	3	4	5	6	7	8	9	10	11	12	13	14	15	16	17	18	19	20	21	22	23	24	25	26	27	28	29	30

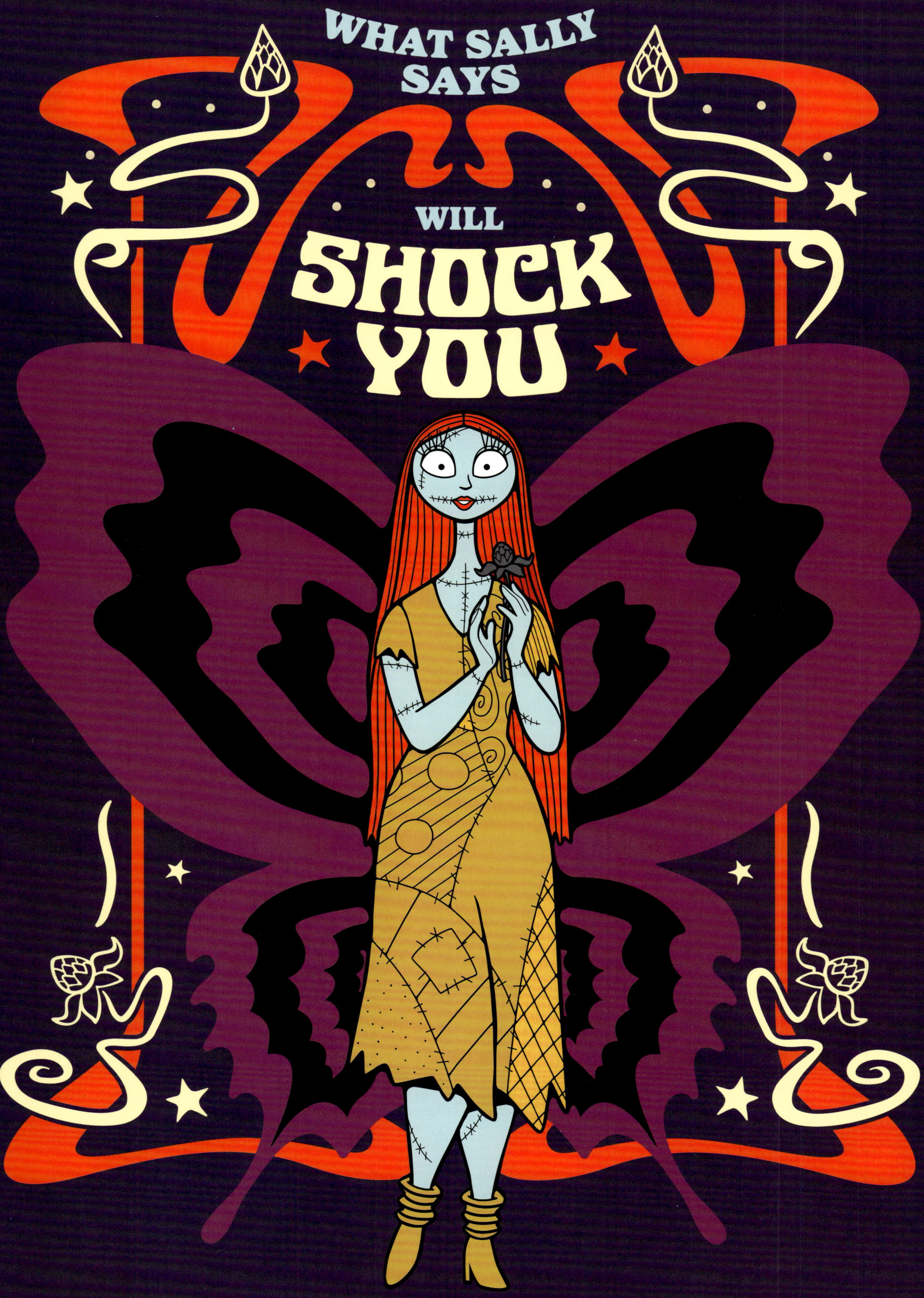
WHAT SALLY SAYS
WILL
SHOCK
YOU

DISNEY
TIM BURTON'S
THE NIGHTMARE BEFORE CHRISTMAS

JULY 2025

NOTABLE DATE: 14 BANK HOLIDAY (NORTHERN IRELAND)

T	W	T	F	S	S	M	T	W	T	F	S	S	M	T	W	T	F	S	S	M	T	W	T	F	S	S	M	T	W	T
1	2	3	4	5	6	7	8	9	10	11	12	13	14	15	16	17	18	19	20	21	22	23	24	25	26	27	28	29	30	31

GET A-HEAD OF THE LINE
FOR THE
ILLUSION
OF A
LIFETIME!

Disney
TIM BURTON'S
THE NIGHTMARE BEFORE CHRISTMAS

AUGUST 2025

NOTABLE DATES: 4 SUMMER BANK HOLIDAY (SCOTLAND) / 25 SUMMER BANK HOLIDAY (ENG, NIR, WAL)

F	S	S	M	T	W	T	F	S	S	M	T	W	T	F	S	S	M	T	W	T	F	S	S	M	T	W	T	F	S	S
1	2	3	4	5	6	7	8	9	10	11	12	13	14	15	16	17	18	19	20	21	22	23	24	25	26	27	28	29	30	31

LET
THE SHOW
BEGIN

Disney
TIM BURTON'S
THE NIGHTMARE BEFORE CHRISTMAS

SEPTEMBER 2025

NOTABLE DATES: 21 INTERNATIONAL DAY OF PEACE (UNITED NATIONS) / 22 ROSH HASHANAH (JEWISH NEW YEAR) BEGINS

M	T	W	T	F	S	S	M	T	W	T	F	S	S	M	T	W	T	F	S	S	M	T	W	T	F	S	S	M	T
1	2	3	4	5	6	7	8	9	10	11	12	13	14	15	16	17	18	19	20	21	22	23	24	25	26	27	28	29	30

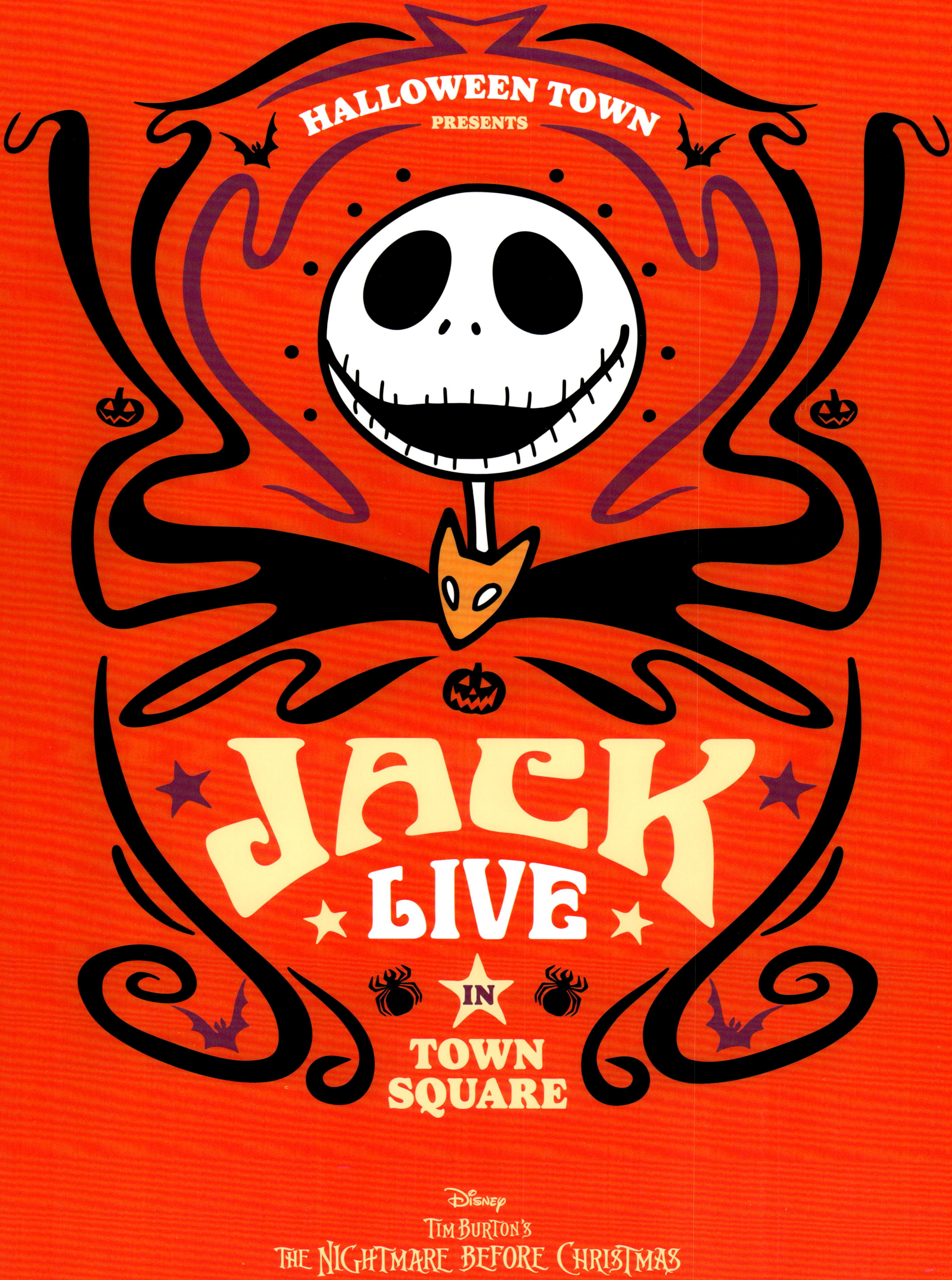

HALLOWEEN TOWN
PRESENTS
JACK
LIVE
IN
TOWN SQUARE
Disney
TIM BURTON'S
THE NIGHTMARE BEFORE CHRISTMAS

OCTOBER 2025

NOTABLE DATES: 1 YOM KIPPUR BEGINS / 10 WORLD MENTAL HEALTH DAY / 20 DIWALI / 26 DAYLIGHT SAVING TIME ENDS / 31 HALLOWEEN

W	T	F	S	S	M	T	W	T	F	S	S	M	T	W	T	F	S	S	M	T	W	T	F	S	S	M	T	W	T	F
1	2	3	4	5	6	7	8	9	10	11	12	13	14	15	16	17	18	19	20	21	22	23	24	25	26	27	28	29	30	31

A FEARFUL
VISION
Disney
TIM BURTON'S
THE NIGHTMARE BEFORE CHRISTMAS

NOVEMBER 2025

NOTABLE DATES: 5 GUY FAWKES NIGHT / 9 REMEMBRANCE SUNDAY / 30 ST. ANDREW'S DAY

S	S	M	T	W	T	F	S	S	M	T	W	T	F	S	S	M	T	W	T	F	S	S	M	T	W	T	F	S	S
1	2	3	4	5	6	7	8	9	10	11	12	13	14	15	16	17	18	19	20	21	22	23	24	25	26	27	28	29	30

KNOW YOUR
DESTINY

Disney
TIM BURTON'S
THE NIGHTMARE BEFORE CHRISTMAS

DECEMBER 2025

NOTABLE DATES: 25 CHRISTMAS DAY / 26 BOXING DAY / 31 NEW YEAR'S EVE

M	T	W	T	F	S	S	M	T	W	T	F	S	S	M	T	W	T	F	S	S	M	T	W	T	F	S	S	M	T	W
1	2	3	4	5	6	7	8	9	10	11	12	13	14	15	16	17	18	19	20	21	22	23	24	25	26	27	28	29	30	31

MAKING CHRISTMAS FRIGHT

Disney
TIM BURTON'S
THE NIGHTMARE BEFORE CHRISTMAS

INCLUDES

TWELVE FRAME-READY PRINTS

EACH IMAGE IS PERFORATED FOR EASY REMOVAL AND PRINTED ON PREMIUM PAPER

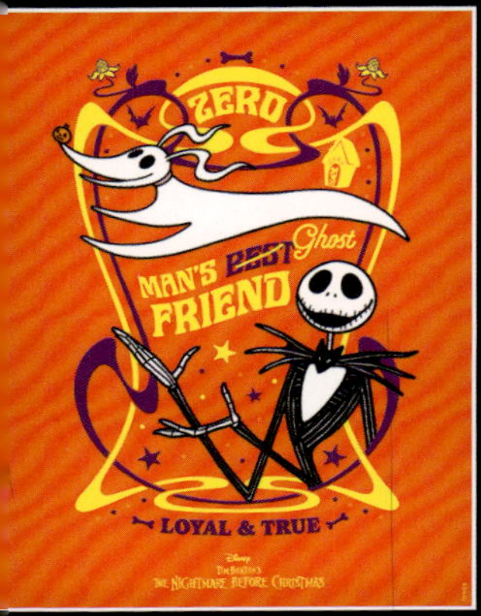

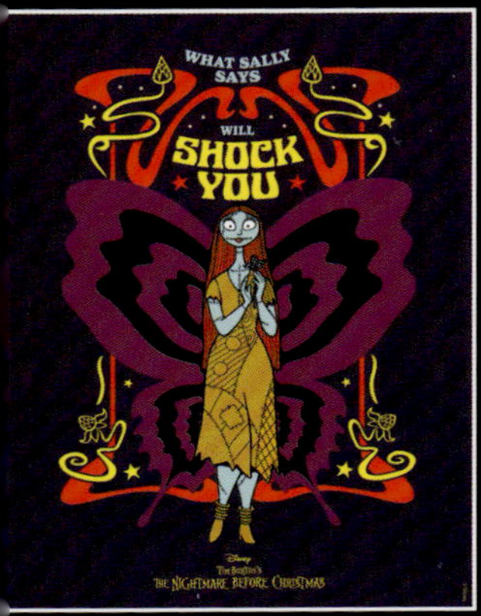

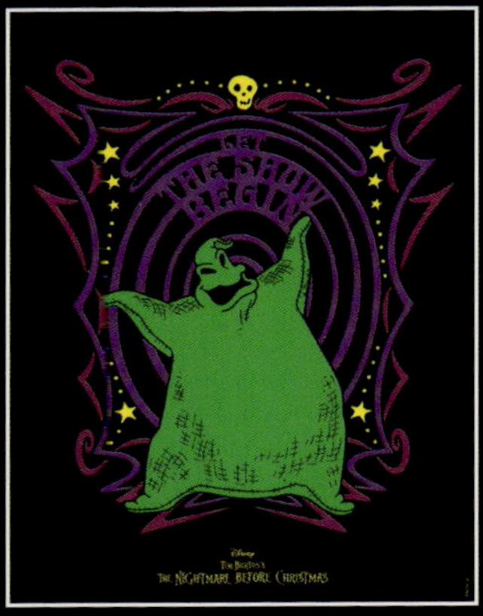

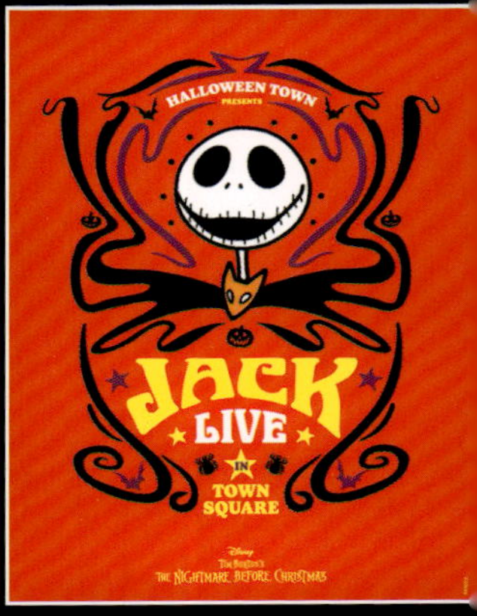

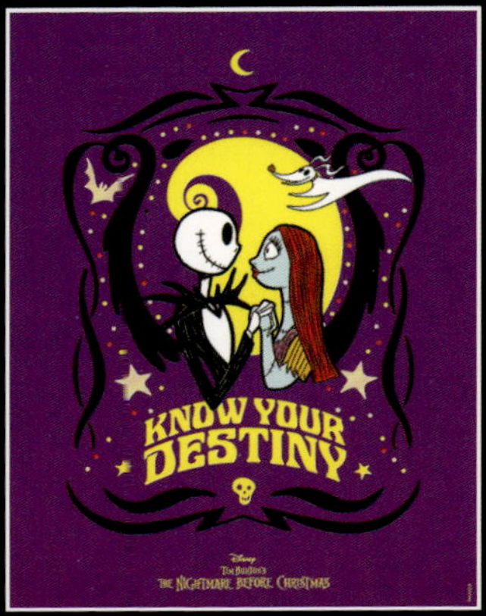

Danilo
WWW.DANILO.COM

Published by Danilo Promotions Ltd. Unit 3,
The io Centre, Lea Road, Waltham Abbey, EN9 1AS, England.
Enquiries: **info@danilo.com**
For all other information: **www.danilo.com**

Printed in China.

While every effort is made to ensure that the information included in this calendar is correct, Danilo Promotions Ltd. cannot be held responsible for errors and omissions. The Banking and Financial Dealings Act, 1971, allows the Government to alter dates at short notice.

Danilo is committed to making all of its products fully recyclable

PAPER Widely Recycled

WIRO Widely Recycled

FSC www.fsc.org MIX Paper from responsible sources FSC® C010609

ISBN 978-1-83527-248-0
ISBN 1-83527-248-7

9 781835 272480